Dearest REBecca!

Happy Happy Birthday

29th ♡ Birthday that is!!!

May this next spin and all future years dancing on Earth Be filled there with the Most exciting, Groovy, delicious, Sexy, romantic, good vibey Times Possible

LOVE LOVE LOVE
HQ Porcaro.

P.S. This is Dear Pal Mandys Work she's Fantastic as are YOU xoxoxo

MATH, HEAVEN, TIME

MANDY KAHN

MATH,
HEAVEN,
TIME

EYEWEAR PUBLISHING

First published in 2014
by Eyewear Publishing Ltd
74 Leith Mansions, Grantully Road
London w9 1LJ
United Kingdom

Typeset with graphic design by Edwin Smet
Author photograph Autumn de Wilde
Printed in England by TJ International Ltd, Padstow, Cornwall

ISBN 978-1-908998-29-3

WWW.EYEWEARPUBLISHING.COM

For Bordo,
with unending thanks

Mandy Kahn is coauthor, with Aaron Rose,
of the book *Collage Culture: Examining the 21st Century's
Identity Crisis* (JRP/Ringier), which is sold in many countries.
She collaborates with composers to create works that feature
poetry in tandem with classical music and has had readings
and signings at Colette (Paris), Motto (Berlin), Shoreditch
House (London), Davies Symphony Hall (San Francisco),
Printed Matter (New York), and Art Center
College of Design (Los Angeles).

Table of Contents

One

Two

Three

One

The Tour Guide

I followed the German tour guide
through the hulking old basilica.

He told the group (or so I guessed),
indicating high and low:

This is where the wind begins.

*This is where the childhoods of a thousand
martyrs live, untouched.*

*Wood grain in these pews still curls
to likenesses of patron saints.*

*Window-holes are cut the breadth
of human souls, when loosed.*

*Dark paint in the frescoes is crushed ants.
White paint is light.*

*Leaves and fauna long extinct are rendered
in the porticoes. See that goat
with antlers? Gone from life,
but captured here.
(Hold your breath and it bows its head.)
(Reach towards the ceiling and sigh, and it sighs.)*

*Worth two times the value of the Bulgar Sea
is that old bell.*

(When younger priests
would ring it,
the nuns were warned to shield their hearts.)

He said far more
I can't recall

and when I tried to pay him,
he spurned my coins, saying, in German,

What good is money,
my child, to the wind?

Poem for Our Ghost

Who can blame the figure
that appeared,
translucent,
glowing, green,
and watched us sleep
just after we'd made love?
Moving
as he does
all night
past rooftops and the tufts of trees,
how could he resist perching closer
to such ardent rest?
Not more now than
lengths of ivy
painted on a scrim, how could he resist
such florid substance, such clay
on clay, two ropes swelled
with ocean water,
bound to the bed,
bound to each other, far as one can get
from his own
estate of
disembodied transit?

Was our fragrance strong enough
to call him down
from his canopy seat in the nighttime?
How long
did he watch us, letting our scented breath
pass heavily through him, how long

did he float,
graceful, ponderous, sad,
before I caught him looking,
where his presence lit the room?
Even I
feel sometimes like a ghost
hovered above us,
trying to get closer,
to become us,
to know for certain our flesh.

Stuck Windows

I don't like having a crush. It makes me
bring my feathers out and loll, hoping
to color the moonlight.
My body disobeys me, my old pal,
now preferring him. When kissed, my shuttered factory
throws open its stuck windows, starting up its clunky gray
machinery to humming, ready to make a new go,
ready to manufacture
whatever it is the kids are buying these days.

Marry Me

1. He Said

I've known women
taught from childhood
all the ways to love a man
further than reason, so he grabs his head
in passion, scared he'll spill his brains,
touched bodies stitched of plum skins, held bodies
shivered thin with fear and sickness
all through sweaty nights,
so near death they stank.
You were not yet born
when I learned for good what a girl could do, and gently,
with flattened hands, looking me straight in the eye.
I'm not here for friendship. I don't want a
lover. Take me to your small house and hang me
like a shelf beside your entryway, water me
and feed me as you see fit. Give me a place to do my work
and I'll show you the finest work of my life, wrap
your legs around me when the day ends and snore.
There, where trash trucks shake the wooden shades
with loud harmonica calls, with your long hands to
shuffle my hair, and finger my toes,
I'll show the world what I can do.

2. She Said

I'm a white Siberian iris
just past seedling
in a vacant lot. Nobody knows
how I got here, how to tend me, how long I'll last.
I'm vulnerable to winds, dropped
temperatures, interruptions, men. To love me
is to watch me from the window
of the tenement across the way, to visit me
on Sundays, to send your prayers. Some things
are so strange to the world, and to themselves, they're best left
to the seasons, which will care for them
in increments so small
they shuffle nothing, impact nothing,
as far as men can see.

What Happened Right Above You

After four days on the satellite, the astronaut turned to his crew.
Space, he said, *is blacker than what's lost,*
blacker than everything piled on top of everything,
blacker than rot, blacker than sludge. It's the path
that winds between us, friends
I've clung to over the edge of this ship, the known,
and over the light, the end.

Now we flip through the films of his past
and find him floating, tethered
to another space suit, fixing his aging ship.
But why do we pause and watch him, hands lost
in the rising gloves, hips lost in a fabric that won't burn
or melt, rationing his breath?
Why do we bother watching? We're all
in love. Who better
knows distance than we.

No Bones

I have no bones.
I'm the windsock
my neighbor forgets
still hangs from his porch.
You can see in the grain of its cloth
where the color was once,
and twice a week
or thereabouts
without a sound
the evening air still lifts it.

Your Hands (Stieglitz to O'Keeffe)

It's not only
they're a pair of starfish wet
on crumbled rock,

or how they're older
than you are,

or that they stand for you:

fingers sometimes square
as cocktail carrots,
and others, round,

fingers sometimes curved in benediction –
woozy with grace –

or flat and spread above your head,
two antennas calling down
through ceiling boards and roof tiles

the next line you will paint. Cleft
of tendon that lifts in your wrist,

lifeline that hints you'll outlive me –

their fluted shape is the leaning shape you always paint,
a drying conch.

It isn't how they always find the light –
or how they're bronze –

how they echo the ditch
that forms by your clavicle –

or how they possess –

how they sneak from the fields of your sleeves
like ferrets,
with a curious nose –

how they're maps of the roads
through the hills by Lake George –

or how they are rakes –

or how each claws his mate, saying: *My love! My foe!*

No. It's
how, holding the tree
in even sunlight,
they are the tree.

Why I Wake Up Slowly

I'm put to sleep, as you are,
by the regular noise of fluttering angels.

With hands the size of nickels
all night they smooth my hair.

When I sleep my deepest
they line the sheets around me
like iridescent dinner plates.
Our breaths, in concert, rise.

Later, just before I wake,
they watch like tiny mothers, hovered
in groups – an air show heard
from many miles away.

I know the sound, and try to stay asleep,
to keep them.

For Edward Weston

You knew you were lucky
to have her: young, not afraid
to strip down straight to flesh and hair
and curve into parentheses, to wishbones,
in the dunes. She didn't fear a week
of finding sand stuck in a knuckle's fold.
She didn't fear your sons, nearly her
age-mates, she didn't fear the former wife
you hadn't quite divorced. Black, flat
anemones in her armpits curved to the light.
Every day you spent with her
was finished, you wondered whether
it mattered, making anything else. Pelted then
by sand, your own desire in waves,
the sun in desolate towns,
you wondered how many ways
a man could possibly come
to love her, or know her,
or see her, or keep her.

The Day My Hall Was Full of Married Men

I call those years the ones that
never stopped. Once I woke to knocking
and a dozen gracious men were in my hallway,
bulging from their shirts. (My roommate, whom I hardly knew,
had called the fire squad, and left.) One man tamed
our flooding sink and many muscled, blushing figures
wove their hands to latticework
and crowded my slight house. Water, which was all I had,
I offered them, and swans
so near to daybreak, they bowed, and searched the floor,
and kindly demurred. Married, most of them, I'm sure,
they turned
from the uncorseted girl in threadbare
striped pyjama pants and ancient shirt that moths
had turned to lace.

Once they'd left, I dressed
for work, and months went by – a year, perhaps –
before I thought of them again:
tasting sleep as they stood shy
of my bare feet, my unswept floor, my battered shirt,
the water that was all I had.

Those years a buzzed excitement
was so steady in my life it was inertia
my body learned to forget. A team of men so clean and thick
and gentle with the words they chose I couldn't even bear to lift
my eyes to them – not past their knees – arriving and bowing
            and leaving so soon,
some morning, having blocked our street – a flock

of sturdy birds touched down in my small pond, then gone
to air – was just another piece of steady motion
in a moving age. There was calm
to them that came from leading worthwhile lives in curtained homes.
Something – more than bulk, than shape – filled
my unwashed rooms. They climbed back on their hulking truck
and went again to risky work. I curled up in the center
of that spinning time and slept for several years.

Ritual for January 1st

Go to the seaside that's balmy all year.
Ask to see the Book of Shale, the Book of Cactus Cut,
the Yarn of Splintered Weather, the Edict of Light
from a Canopied Moon. Walk among the beach rocks with
            that stack of texts
set flush on your head, then gather up the soft spots
in your softening mind and push one hand through. It's warm inside,
when you're up to your wrist; when you've lost a whole arm,
            you've gained two.
Flex and curl each finger in that curious deep: it springs back new.
What feels like sponges is water, what feels like water is rest,
what feels like rest to the flat of your palm
is efficiency and health and nerve. Let what happens
happen to you, then pull yourself out
by the suck of a breath. The year you'll enter, after that,
will cradle your feet like river mud, and you'll speak to it
with a curious, tea-wet mouth.

Math, Heaven, Time

Math, the thing I couldn't manage,
time, the thing I, harried, chased,
heaven, the place I couldn't posit could exist.

Math, the thing I build with, these days,
time, the well I can't drink dry,
heaven, the place my body walks inside, and toward.

Years are towers built on other years.
Truth is fabric sewn from scraps
you come upon. Rock can sigh to sand.

Two

To Amanda Prynne, From Elyot Chase, in Tunis

Another month without our shoes,
with oysters in their bowls of ice,
sucking out their spongy meat
and wiping down our chins. Nothing in *The Times* is new,
they bring it with our lunch,
people that we know have gotten married
or divorced, or both. Hannis brings a round of drinks,
knowing what we'll want. Puffins
winging soundless at the shore
are just the gnats in Kent.

I knew you
in your pigtails, in loafers, at Charing Cross,
I knew you when your cheeks were white as aphids,
when your skirts were smocked. Never was there
choosing to be done by us, my clotted cream,
my ice cubes in a glass of scotch, my cricket afternoons.
The wordlessness between us now, let me just be clear,
was due us from the cradle, we were fed for it, we were raised
for it. Our hands were stitched from grass to fit
in holding. I learned words to say these.

For James

Now he leaves her penciled notes where figures,
swarmed by wavy lines, consider the rules of the physical world
with evident bewilderment. *How should I proceed*, one thinks,
reaching up stick hands, *knowing you're off eating lamb
and drinking port with what's-his-face? Now,*
begins another figure, this one on an ample chair,
I spend mornings breaking wax from candlesticks, or skipping stones.

*You looked to me, at Thursday's brunch, like
Cleopatra sitting for her portrait,* says a thick-browed figure
cradling his head.

He comes to fix her drawer,
hang up a shelf, and leaves a dozen more,
in all her folded socks: *Try porridge – it's good eating,
Never visit Philly in high August,
Vinegar plus water cleans most things.*

The note she never gives him –
she's drawn herself as circle over triangle, with lines
for legs, no features on her face – says,
*The roots of trees
by Puffer's Pond in Sunderland, Ohio
crowd along its sandy banks like earthworms,
though its bed is dry.*

Room 15

Morning lasts till afternoon
in that hotel.

I was on the terrace; in the dog-eared
book, Jeeves triumphed again.

The sleeping man inside
was breathing heavy as a shore of seals.

In due course, we'd have breakfast,
that sleeping man and I,
with pots of tea, and talk,
and scones,
and read *The New York Times*.

But first he slept for hours,
carelessly, in perfect dark;

I waited,
as brand-new lovers,
interlopers,
castle-builders,
do.

At the Dorm

Week upon week at the dorm she watched him
working at a table with a pencil in his teeth,
eating with a stack of books and papers,
reading while he walked. His hair was
groups of angry men, his sweaty cuffs were wrinkled
at his forearms: he seemed to be loved by no one.
But always there were pairs of houseflies
hovering above him, landing on his nest of notes,
trailing him as if with streamers and sound.
A farm girl, she knew to follow the flies:
they'll take you to the milk just pulled to the pail,
to the cow's haunch where the meat will one day be sweetest,
the swelled pond, the unlatched gate. Everything,
she knew, was in those notebooks
he would carry: her future, the distances of islands, poles
and stars, the reason for the network of men's follies,
how to spend the night.

My Heart Is a House Where Nobody Lives

I wouldn't even know the way
to make love now.
If anyone tried, I'd cleave
like the bulbs of a cell when it's splitting.
If anyone tried, I'd separate,
beside myself.

I was the one that everyone loved
yet ended up lonely.
That makes me a miraculous feat of loneliness.
They said my loneliness couldn't be done
and I went and showed them.
In the world of loneliness, everyone knows my name.

Seventeen Girls

Seventeen girls at the seashore
eating cake.

The corners of that memory are a blinding white,
from ogling that scene.

(It hurt to look, or breathe.)

What matters is that I was wrong
about those girls: I thought
seventeen locked dressers, I thought
all those rivers I will never ford.

But ford I did, that fragrant girl, that nest of dill –
that memory's cut from slate.

(Only stone you've held has weight.)

To the Couples Who Argue on Reality TV

Try to keep in mind:

she's a scarlet crane, extinct in the wild,
here only
by the grace of several zoos, and at a
staggering cost, so the world
will not yet lose her –

and he, he is a houseboat loaded up for
many seasons, flying streamers,
trailing a league of minnows.

Ron Pulls Pans

Ron pulls pans from the stove, browned yams
with quartered beets, and one of yellow squash. Frank's in town
from lonely Taos, we cheer him,

Millie Sterkel, sans her father, comes up from downstairs.

Drawings hang around the walls
on fraying string by clothes pins
and Millie makes a drawing of a massive fern with wings for leaves.
She'll grow up thinking all adults
spend evenings talking, drawing, grouped,
decorating flimsy walls with buckshot from their
heads. Night
gets cold and comes inside when Frank goes out to smoke,
Millie offers up her toy: glasses that dissolve the light.

The dinner's many colors
are a prism in my body: they're breaking me to my component parts.

The glasses do their job.

Most days we work to put to sleep the palettes that reside in light.
I give myself this fracture –
the colored wings that sprout from heavy forms,
as decks of cards are spread.
My ears are full of talking,
I taste beets –

the box that contains me is thin.

Always, It Is Afternoon

In Case Study House #20, a tree grows through the roof.
A stationary panel makes the breakfast room distinct from the living.
A fire's always burning and a woman's always waiting
with a tray, in heels and earrings, through filmy sliding doors.

Coolness renders beauty
in a place like this: books all pushed to the edge of their shelves,
on which no more would fit,
no gadgets with their cords and sounds and several signals floating.
No socks on the bedroom floor
as if their feet had melted.
Nothing but a bowl of waxy apples
and a hanging lamp.

Perhaps inside this gallery our last words to each other
are spoken in restrained tones by actors on a loop.
The one playing you might lounge by the pool with his knees up,
        shading his eyes,
the one playing me might float on her back, supporting her head
        with her hands.

Nothing comes to any sense where square bricks
make the curved face of a fireplace,
where moving chairs scuff nothing, where bread won't crumb.
The leaning pine that splits the scene might make each side a capsule.
The shadow that the old pine throws might swing across us slowly,
to no effect.

The Sound

The goats lower their craggy beards
to clover
from their fondness
when the farmer comes, with pails
of heavy slop. What they leak
is simple: ripe devotion.
It swells them like warm lanterns.
Their heads sag to their hooves
when it is too much.

This year, for the first time,
their eyes are bad. Their dear,
their slim deliverer
of day-old loaves
and rotting pears
and steady strokes to neck and flank
and shoulder blade
is this year only sound:
rain boots through knee-high grass,
the zipping of ribbed strands,
the metered, tired, prudent pace
of climbers. And o,
the splash of lavish sludge, with corn,
against the pail –
the sound of day achieving itself, of day
being cut into morning and night,
the sound of coming heaviness
of belly, the body's greed abated,
the naps in beds of clover that will come.

We

Suddenly the tulips
have turned down –
they eye the table now like
girls stunned at their faces in a pond.
An hour ago they roved the air like Saturns
in their orbitals,
circling their heavy vase,
measuring the day. But then they drained their bowl,
too soon. Summer came on hot, and fast.

You and I keep water in our bowl,
filling, filling,
quick to be the one who fixes dinner, clears and
washes plates, says the gentle thing
into the other's neck, pets the other's hair.
We can stretch so tall, two aspens,
trunks that only grow one way. How one's back can learn to stretch
like aspens, one's roots to spread, to seek.

Edges

The doctor sends a tincture
that will mix with the water inside me
and bubble into thin industrious steam.
Some organ will endure its clogged ducts cleaned.
Agents will move through me
with agendas, adept and light.

I'll see then what I've failed to see,
not colors but their edges, not seasons but the many points in snow.
I'll understand your leaving, and what I said, and what I failed to say.
From the seat of this better machinery
I'll lose you again, but sharper.
The face of every building will display its tiles and boards.

I'd rather let a skin form on the pudding by the mixer,
let dust build on the cactus pot, let spiders drop, let curtains fringe.
I'd rather leave the crayons on the back seat of the hot car,
spreading into one imperfect being, with all their very wax.

Three

Very Long Haiku

On the way to someplace else
we pulled off a road in Kansas
and peed in a wheat field.
This was ten years ago and I've failed to describe it many times since.
Midnight was nearing, the wheat was glowing: grass
in an underwater cave.
It was soft on our arms.
We parted it.
We went in separate directions, into the wheat, to offer each other
            privacy.

The smell of that wheat was something to pitch a tent and live inside.
We'd barely spoken in days, from some grudge.
We spoke of the smell of that wheat.

How to Solve

Put tulips in the middle of the problem.
Don't clean if you can't. Don't eat
if you cannot bear the smell. Put tulips
on the table, beside the mail
and papers and coupons and trash.
Tomorrow when you wake between discordant dreams discordant,
you'll see their heads
stretched nimbly towards a gravel-speckled moon:
a race on pause,
a team of sperm forever in pursuit.

The papers will eventually right themselves. You'll rise one day
and process them or papers will arrive
that won't need signing.
The point is not the flowers without the papers.
The point is not the papers plus the flowers.
A bright spot tempts the flowers and your ancient speakers leak
      a clear sonata.
Breathe, then stretch, a tulip,
toward your body's love.

All My Years Wear Matching Coats

All my years wear matching coats
and line up, staring out to sea.
There! says one. *A ship! Its prow!*
Quite! says another. *Wind at its back.*
Here! calls a third, waving its hands.
A fourth lights a flare and a fifth puts it out.
What, says the fifth, *would any of us*
do anymore, if a ship saw that?

American Poem

Let's forget our debt
in each other's arms.
The leaning house is quiet now, those peeling walls
we strain each month to own.
Our parents look at us with disappointment.
They say it wasn't hard to pay their owed.
All we have
is the breath in our ears from each other,
and places where our skin is not too stretched.
All we have are the free things: the pond
in March, its bottom muck, the path
that leads to bottom muck through ferns. Those things should
have been enough – the too-abundant things.
Our lives will be protracted now
and strained. Our love
will be strained. The pipes at night
make an old sound, so we know they are strained.
Nightfall takes its place in sheets
around our empire. It lays us flat.
We dream of closets empty.

The Woman Who Values the Possible Most

If she could, the potter, slight
and curved like a branch that ends in fruit,
would throw a pot so big
a couch and bed would fit inside,
and top it
with a dried clay slab, a pan's lid, and sleep there,
so when it rained
she'd wake at night
and find it smelled again
the way it smelled the morning
it was a lump in her hands.

Waiting

It's been ten years already of waiting.
It might take another ten years.
The lake does not grow colder, the boat floats off
with no driver aboard and moss is sunning bodies
on the stones.

Hard as the waiting has been,
maybe having will be harder,
or maybe it's hardest being the lake
while it's waiting to be earned. Brick by brick
I build the skiff that will take me,
hoping it will float.

Snapshot

It's been said of William Eggleston
you're his best friend
if you're in the room.

I was once his best friend.
What a room.

Poem for Nan Goldin

I've always had trouble turning the page
past Nan Goldin's photograph 'Breakfast in Bed'

because coffee and a basket of buns

and a second basket, of clustered fruit,
and a hard-boiled egg standing in an egg cup,

and matched floral china, and various spoons,
across a rumpled coverlet

at a hotel somewhere in Florence seems reward enough
for this uncertain life. Termites tucked in everything,

then everything tented, everything sprayed,
everything left by the side of the road then purchased again,
perpetually: years of this

are easier with the image of breakfast

placed on bedding ridged the way
two grappling bodies leave it ridged,

cup still full and coffee warm, creamed
to the color of coconut skin,
woven napkins folded by saucers

and curtains pulled apart:

there's a door in the wall, there's a knob on the door,
there's a key in the lock, then finally

an egg that's been boiled and stands, cooled,
near its very own spoon, waiting to be peeled.

Poem That Straddles the Globe

And who are you, stopped below my window,
playing songs in Gaelic? That cowbell of a voice,
damp with pastures, hangs like soggy skirts.
Are you here in Echo Park,
carbound, with a rocking wheel,
while someone knits a hat for you
for Christmas, over Irish stew?
I've lived two places too, toe
in the ocean, head on a plane. I've let my body
be a coat, my soul a small balloon. A man can live
that way for many seasons, as you may know.
No one understands a word you say,
but you're just a coat.

Why There Are Dishes Growing Scales in My Wet Kitchen Sink

Several cords still snake across my bedroom: they are cracks.
I've planned for many seasons
how I'd tack them to the molding, to clear the floor,
and once a month, while dreaming,
I do. But cracks are strings
that hold us to the earth: I know that if we filled them,
we'd turn to doves and rise through steam
to claim our promised place within eternity.
I worry for those people in their renovated lofts,
with perfectly painted corners and evenly grouted tile:
what keeps each of them
from shifting into air? I'm made of clay
because bags of things to be organized
still line my entryway. (I like the smell of mopping floors
but I stop before I'm done.)
(A person with so much left to prove
tethers herself to the living.)

Over Our Bones

Under our skin, over our bones there's a
white, pliable sheet we call our fascia.
Mine, explains the doctor,
has gone tough.
My chiropractor, later,
calls it a ghost: a gummy web made tight by what
we've been through, that holds things fast.
Now I stretch all morning, fingers on
the soiled edge of a door frame. I make my shoulders
hang me, a ship's curved prow.

And now some days
I feel them come unstuck: old times.
Those arid years a heavy wind
could have lifted me, the small thin sail of me, and now
those years are a small thin sail within me, a sail
I'm learning how to twist, a sail that's
starting to give. I'm warming something up, from ore:
the statue of a yearling,
its head bowed,
its ears back,
trying to be good.

Man Ray

Sometimes we can't guess
what we'll become, or what
we are. Man Ray
thought himself a painter,
time has favored his photographs.
Maybe it's a lot of smoke
and mirrors, all this wanting to be.
Better to throw the mailbag
of your life's work into history,
all its letters written in a careful hand,
envelopes still sealed.

Fish on a Plate

Isn't it strange, dog on a leash, fish on a plate, flag flapping?
Seems that I've run off and done it again, possibly better this time,
maybe worse. Child with a flag, fish on a leash,
maybe I've learned nothing, but if I could bundle
this bundle of nothing and give it to you, you'd gape.
Flap on a dog, plate on a flag, leash on a child,
fish slapping: nothing and nothing is nothing again, but
glorious in its lapping. Take up the bugle, wrap up the violets
in crinoline paper, start packing. The nothing I've learned
makes an excellent quiet for hearing: start snapping.

Why I Don't Bother Raising My Voice

I've reached the point in the novel
where I'm Scrooge, wanting my actual life,
that kitchen scrap I've brushed aside for years.
But what does she hear, the girl behind glass
I call to, while the third ghost leans his scythe?
My breath can't raise the hair
from her delicate forearms, and she'll do
and she'll do what she'll do.

The Teenage Runaway's Late-day Prayer

Too hot for work, a sandwich going gluey
in her gut,
she stretches out to nap her way to evening,
and to pray. In pebbled dark made pinstriped
by slatted blinds that won't go flat
she looks up at the pock marks
in the ceiling and exhales.
Nothing that is hers is hers alone. She's daughter
of a gracious, loping graciousness, she knows –
truant from a town of ruts and horseflies,
fallow dirt and dread. To those she knows, she wishes health,
creamy drinks from blenders in the evenings,
flowering Japanese trees.
Then a napping comes to her,
mounting her with choirboys in heavy robes
clustered together on horseback.
She follows on a pebbled mare,
through thicket, which is wet as peat,
where moss hangs fat and fragrant,
where mushrooms rise like cakes.

Several-month Vacation

Sometimes you wrap up your life in brown paper,
tie it with string and leave it behind.
(I've taken up my skirt hem
and stepped into the afternoon.) You cannot know
for certain it will be there
when you've wandered home. You leave
as a head on a body – the body leaves, you ride.
A horseman, you hover your heels
by the stirrups, waiting to see what you'll do.

Hours Passed

Hours passed. The princess, tired,
slovenly now from rending her scarves, leaned
from the end of her doe's-leg neck a curious face,
right through the slit in the door. *Time*, she reminded us,
is a necklace smelling of garlic, made of bronze cubes,
sewn into your breastplate: it's a boil.
She didn't show her face again for a week, and then it was
cottony, changed.
I've nothing to do, she told us, and eyeballed
each one plainly. *The shapes have peeled from my curtains*
and my parrot has eaten my finch. Where is the giant wave pool
bobbed with lanterns that will carry me to sea?

I met her again
at a bistro, by chance, after her father was ousted. The peacefulness
in her shoulders was new and she moved with the air
like a sail. *Still*
I've finished zilch, she said, and puffed a slim cigar.
But now that I'm all wrinkled, I'm able to enter a room
without commotion, and
that fixes things. That fixes things
enough.

The Clock We Use in Echo Park

This one's for the rooster
that crows for dawn all day
from a coop I cannot locate
somewhere on my block. He knows
that night is afternoon, that afternoon
is dawn, that daybreak
is a shawl you wear across your shoulders
into night.
When I miss a deadline
he tells me deadlines never come: we live in them,
they cannot be without us, we're their very love, their breath.

Mrs. Mary Good

1.

Stinking from the sty, Nils tries to love me.
He tends those pigs like they were kin.
He likes those pigs too much.
I hear them grunting from their pens
from noon till noon,
an acre past the shed.

He's up at dawn, and I'm up too, boiling
coffee water. Too handsome
for such dirty work: cheeks still white as they were
in town, when even deep behind his ears
it was lemony. The room he leased, kept
swept and straight, was quiet all the hours of night.
Nils, I'd say. *My Nils*. Now I fold the note,
make up the bed, fill my canvas bag. I'll sleep till half past noon
wherever I land next, by Jove. I leave him for the pigs: bowed now
with his pair of pails, crossing shin-high grass –

my husband – Nils – my slop king –
my dirt-caked reed –
my slender muddy stream.

2.

Years can't change a person that you haven't seen.
Decades pass, and still:
Nils is at the bedroom door, the smell of pig
an orbiting confetti.

The intervening husbands have been acres
filled with grass and air –
quiet dells to do my sewing,
wet in the mornings, lush in the rain.

He's
mounting pigpen riots in the distance,
scarcely twenty still,
blond as water, balancing full pails.

Poem That Contains All Time

A sheep encountered a fisherman
in rags
near the edge of the world.

Why, inquired the sheep, *even now,*
do you cast your line? The day
is all but over and the fish
have learned to outsmart you.

The fisherman spoke with a crack
in his affable voice. *Soft thing*, he said.

You're a place to rest one's ear
after months of crunching leaves
with muddy boots. You're what will turn

a vicious day to dream, what launches us
to buckshot, what ties night to our eyes,
you're the door in the wall.

You're the pack —
a bag of cotton balls,

an acre of clasped hands. But also you're
a single thread, which, pried from its grid,

with little force unwinds the sheet
we've knitted to a pile.

Your grouped brain is the one that asks
this question. The other brain –

the stalk of wheat just dug up
from the cooling field –

already knows: even when the stream
is free of beasts, when yellowed grass

appears in clumps so thick the water
can't loop through and, fretting, dries,

the fisherman carries his tackle box
to the dust bowl where the river ends,

casts his line, unwraps his lunch and sits.
An eon is a lot of time
to wait for a change in weather, but forever
is a longer time, and a single day with an unstrung pole
to a man as old as I am
is a broken watch, a swath of cactus needles: all time.

Notes

'Your Hands (Stieglitz to O'Keeffe)': This poem concerns the many photographs that Alfred Stieglitz took of the hands of his partner, the painter Georgia O'Keeffe. Stieglitz's portraits of O'Keeffe are collected in the book *Georgia O'Keeffe: A Portrait by Alfred Stieglitz*.

'For Edward Weston': At age 48, photographer Edward Weston began a romantic relationship with 20-year-old Charis Wilson, whom he later married. Many of Weston's most iconic images are nudes of Wilson, including a series of Wilson in the Oceano Dunes.

'To Amanda Prynne, From Elyot Chase, in Tunis': Amanda Prynne and Elyot Chase are characters – both British – in Noël Coward's play *Private Lives*. They were married to each other once but they divorced; at the start of the play, each is newly remarried. Much of their dialogue is spent debating whether they should leave their spouses and run off together, and ultimately they do. This poem imagines that the pair ends up in Tunis, and is set there a few months after the play's action ends.

'Always, It Is Afternoon': This poem concerns photographer Julius Shulman's images of Case Study House #20, a mid-century modern home built in 1958 for a family called Bass.

Acknowledgements

'The Tour Guide', 'Stuck Windows' and 'Poem That Contains All Time' originally appeared in the journal *The Rattling Wall*. They are reprinted here with thanks to that journal's editors.

EYEWEAR PUBLISHING